Words for my Princess

From Dad

ISBN: 1519649223
ISBN-13: 9781519649225

I was the first man to
unconditionally love you.
And I will love you until my last
day.
This is my words to you.
My words of love.
When you are lonely, sad,
heartbroken and need your dad,
then read this.
With this journal I will always
be with you.
I love you.

Dedication

From Dad

From Dad

From Dad

From Dad

From Dad

From Dad

From Dad

From Dad

From Dad

From Dad

At the end there is only love.

Be strong.

Be the woman I raised you to be.

Love Dad

www.ingramcontent.com/pod-product-compliance
Lightning Source LLC
Chambersburg PA
CBHW050520290526
45786CB00007B/2631
* 9 7 8 1 5 1 9 6 4 9 2 2 5 *